LIFE
Lessons
WITH MAX LUCADO

Pat Frank
272-7255

BOOK OF
1 CORINTHIANS

A SPIRITUAL HEALTH CHECK-UP

MAX LUCADO

Prepared by
THE LIVINGSTONE CORPORATION

THOMAS NELSON
Since 1798

NASHVILLE   DALLAS   MEXICO CITY   RIO DE JANEIRO

D0057770

Life Lessons with Max Lucado— Book of 1 Corinthians

Copyright © by Thomas Nelson, 2007

Published in Nashville, Tennessee. Thomas Nelson is a trademark of Thomas Nelson, Inc..

Thomas Nelson, Inc. titles may be purchased in bulk for educational, business, fundraising, or sales promotional use. For information, please email SpecialMarkets@ThomasNelson.com.

Produced with the assistance of the Livingstone Corporation (www.livingstonecorp.com). Project staff include Jake Barton, Joel Bartlett, Andy Culbertson, Mary Horner Collins, and Will Reaves.

Editor: Neil Wilson

Scripture quotations marked "NCV™" are taken from the New Century Version®. Copyright © 2005 by Thomas Nelson, Inc. Used by permission. All rights reserved.

Scripture quotations marked "NKJV™" are taken from the New King James Version®. Copyright © 1982 by Thomas Nelson, Inc. Used by permission. All rights reserved.

Scripture quotations marked (NIV) are taken from the Holy Bible, New International Version. Copyright © 1973, 1978, 1984 by International Bible Society. All rights reserved. Used by permission of Zondervan Publishing House.

Scripture quotations marked (TLB) are taken from from *The Living Bible*, copyright © 1971. Used by permission of Tyndale House Publishers, Inc., P.O. Box 80, Wheaton, Illinois 60189.

Scripture quotations marked (GNT) are taken from the Good News Bible in Today's English Version, Second Edition. Copyright © 1992 by American Bible Society. Used by permission. All rights reserved.

Material for the "Inspiration" sections taken from the following books:

God Came Near. Copyright © 2004 by Max Lucado. W Publishing Group, a Division of Thomas Nelson, Inc., Nashville, Tennessee.

The Great House of God. Copyright © 1997 by Max Lucado. W Publishing Group, a Division of Thomas Nelson, Inc., Nashville, Tennessee.

In the Eye of the Storm. Copyright © 1991 by Max Lucado. W Publishing Group, a Division of Thomas Nelson, Inc., Nashville, Tennessee.

It's Not About Me. Copyright © 2004 by Max Lucado. Integrity Publishers, Brentwood, Tennessee.

Just Like Jesus. Copyright © 2003 by Max Lucado. W Publishing Group, a Division of Thomas Nelson, Inc., Nashville, Tennessee.

A Love Worth Giving. Copyright 2002 by Max Lucado, W Publishing Group, a Division of Thomas Nelson, Nashville, Tennessee.

No Wonder They Call Him the Savior. Copyright © 1986, 2004 by Max Lucado. W Publishing Group, a Division of Thomas Nelson, Inc., Nashville, Tennessee.

Traveling Light. Copyright © 2001 by Max Lucado. W Publishing Group, a Division of Thomas Nelson, Inc., Nashville, Tennessee.

When God Whispers Your Name. Copyright © 1994, 1999 by Max Lucado. W Publishing Group, a Division of Thomas Nelson, Inc., Nashville, Tennessee.

Cover Art by Kirk Luttrell of the Livingstone Corporation

Composition by Rachel Hawkins of the Livingstone Corporation

ISBN-10: 1-4185-0947-7

ISBN-13: 978-1-4185-0947-7

LIFE *Lessons*

WITH MAX LUCADO

CONTENTS

HOW TO STUDY THE BIBLE

This is a peculiar book you are holding. Words crafted in another language. Deeds done in a distant era. Events recorded in a far-off land. Counsel offered to a foreign people. This is a peculiar book.

It's surprising that anyone reads it. It's too old. Some of its writings date back five thousand years. It's too bizarre. The book speaks of incredible floods, fires, earthquakes, and people with supernatural abilities. It's too radical. The Bible calls for undying devotion to a carpenter who called himself God's Son.

Logic says this book shouldn't survive. Too old, too bizarre, too radical.

The Bible has been banned, burned, scoffed, and ridiculed. Scholars have mocked it as foolish. Kings have branded it as illegal. A thousand times over the grave has been dug and the dirge has begun, but somehow the Bible never stays in the grave. Not only has it survived; it has thrived. It is the single most popular book in all of history. It has been the best-selling book in the world for years!

There is no way on earth to explain it. Which perhaps is the only explanation. The answer? The Bible's durability is not found on earth; it is found in heaven. For the millions who have tested its claims and claimed its promises, there is but one answer: the Bible is God's book and God's voice.

As you read it, you would be wise to give some thought to two questions. What is the purpose of the Bible? and How do I study the Bible? Time spent reflecting on these two issues will greatly enhance your Bible study.

What is the purpose of the Bible?

Let the Bible itself answer that question.

Since you were a child you have known the Holy Scriptures which are able to make you wise. And that wisdom leads to salvation through faith in Christ Jesus. (2 Tim. 3:15 NCV)

The purpose of the Bible? Salvation. God's highest passion is to get his children home. His book, the Bible, describes his plan of salvation. The purpose of the Bible is to proclaim God's plan and passion to save his children.

That is the reason this book has endured through the centuries. It dares to tackle the toughest questions about life: Where do I go after I die? Is there a God? What do I do with my fears? The Bible offers answers to these crucial questions. It is the treasure map that leads us to God's highest treasure—eternal life.

But how do we use the Bible? Countless copies of Scripture sit unread on bookshelves and nightstands simply because people don't know how to read it. What can we do to make the Bible real in our lives?

The clearest answer is found in the words of Jesus. He promised:

Ask, and God will give to you. Search, and you will find. Knock, and the door will open for you. (Matt. 7:7 NCV)

The first step in understanding the Bible is asking God to help us. We should read prayerfully. If anyone understands God's Word, it is because of God and not the reader.

But the Helper will teach you everything and will cause you to remember all that I told you. The Helper is the Holy Spirit whom the Father will send in my name. (John 14:26 NCV)

Before reading the Bible, pray. Invite God to speak to you. Don't go to Scripture looking for your idea; go searching for his.

Not only should we read the Bible prayerfully; we should read it carefully. *Search and you will find* is the pledge. The Bible is not a newspaper to be skimmed but rather a mine to be quarried.

Search for it like silver, and hunt for it like hidden treasure. Then you will understand respect for the LORD, and you will find that you know God. (Prov. 2:4–5 NCV)

Any worthy find requires effort. The Bible is no exception. To understand the Bible you don't have to be brilliant, but you must be willing to roll up your sleeves and search.

Be a worker who is not ashamed and who uses the true teaching in the right way. (2 Tim. 2:15 NCV)

Here's a practical point. Study the Bible a bit at a time. Hunger is not satisfied by eating twenty-one meals in one sitting once a week. The body needs a steady diet to remain strong. So does the soul. When God sent food to his people in the wilderness, he didn't provide loaves already made. Instead, he sent them manna in the shape of *"thin flakes like frost . . . on the desert ground"* (Ex. 16:14 NCV).

God gave manna in limited portions. God sends spiritual food the same way. He opens the heavens with just enough nutrients for today's hunger. He provides *"a command here, a command there. A rule here, a rule there. A little lesson here, a little lesson there"* (Isa. 28:10 NCV).

Don't be discouraged if your reading reaps a small harvest. Some days a lesser portion is all that is needed. What is important is to search every day for that day's message. A steady diet of God's Word over a lifetime builds a healthy soul and mind.

A little girl returned from her first day at school. Her mom asked, "Did you learn anything?"

"Apparently not enough," the girl responded, "I have to go back tomorrow and the next day and the next . . ."

Such is the case with learning. And such is the case with Bible study. Understanding comes little by little over a lifetime.

There is a third step in understanding the Bible. After the asking and seeking comes the knocking. After you ask and search, then knock.

Knock, and the door will open for you. (Matt. 7:7 NCV)

To knock is to stand at God's door. To make yourself available. To climb the steps, cross the porch, stand at the doorway, and volunteer. Knocking goes beyond the realm of thinking and into the realm of acting.

To knock is to ask, What can I do? How can I obey? Where can I go?

It's one thing to know what to do. It's another to do it. But for those who do it, those who choose to obey, a special reward awaits them.

The truly happy are those who carefully study God's perfect law that makes people free, and they continue to study it. They do not forget what they heard, but they obey what God's teaching says. Those who do this will be made happy. (James 1:25 NCV)

What a promise. Happiness comes to those who do what they read! It's the same with medicine. If you only read the label but ignore the pills, it won't help. It's the same with food. If you only read the recipe but never cook, you won't be fed. And it's the same with the Bible. If you only read the words but never obey, you'll never know the joy God has promised.

Ask. Search. Knock. Simple, isn't it? Why don't you give it a try? If you do, you'll see why you are holding the most remarkable book in history.

INTRODUCTION TO THE BOOK OF 1 CORINTHIANS

An Indian was walking up a mountain when he heard a voice.

"Carry me with you," it requested.

The Indian turned and saw a snake. He refused. "If I carry you up the mountain, you will bite me."

"I wouldn't do that," the snake assured. "All I need is some help. I am slow, and you are fast; please be kind and carry me to the top of the mountain."

It was against his better judgment, but the Indian agreed. He picked up the snake, put him in his shirt, and resumed the journey. When they reached the top, he reached in his shirt to remove the snake and got bit. He fell to the ground, and the snake slithered away.

"You lied!" the Indian cried. "You said you wouldn't bite me."

The snake stopped and looked back, "I didn't lie. You knew who I was when you picked me up."

We hear the legend and shake our heads. He should have known better, we bemoan. And we are right. He should have. And so should we. But don't we do the same? Don't we believe the lies of the snake? Don't we pick up what we should leave alone?

The Corinthian Christians did. One snake after another had hissed lies in their ears, and they had believed it. How many lies did they believe? How much time do you have?

The list is long and ugly: sectarianism, disunity, sexual immorality. And that is only the first six chapters. But the book of 1 Corinthians is more than a list of sins; it is an epistle of patience. Paul initiates the letter by calling these Christians "brothers." He could have called them heretics or hypocrites or skirt-chasers, and in so many words he does, but not before he calls them brothers.

He patiently teaches them about worship, unity, the role of women, and the Lord's Supper. He writes as if he can see them face-to-face. He is disturbed but not despondent. Angry but not desperate. His driving passion is love. And his treatise on love in chapter 13 remains the greatest essay ever penned.

The letter, however personal, is not just for Corinth. It is for all who have heard the whisper and felt the fangs. We, like the Indian, should have known better. We, like the Corinthians, sometimes need a second chance.

THE FOOLISHNESS OF HUMAN WISDOM

MAX LUCADO

REFLECTION

Some things don't change. Today, as in Paul's day, believing in Jesus is often a stumbling block for people. People label the gospel message as too simple, too unbelievable, or too unrealistic. It isn't what people want to believe. They want to believe something that they can claim to have discovered, created, or invented. But the gospel is God's idea. That's why it seems so strange to human beings. Which aspects of the gospel (Jesus' life, death, and resurrection) do you think are hard for the modern mind to understand and accept?

SITUATION

The apostle Paul begins this first of several letters to the church in Corinth with compliments and concerns. He has heard about their amazing potential and their disheartening divisions. The church is a house divided, and Paul knows they will not stand if they remain that way. He pleads for their unity in Christ.

BOOK OF 1 CORINTHIANS

OBSERVATION

Read 1 Corinthians 1:18–31 from the NCV or the NKJV.

NCV

18The teaching about the cross is foolishness to those who are being lost, but to us who are being saved it is the power of God. 19It is written in the Scriptures:

"I will cause the wise men to lose their wisdom;

I will make the wise men unable to understand."

20Where is the wise person? Where is the educated person? Where is the skilled talker of this world? God has made the wisdom of the world foolish. 21In the wisdom of God the world did not know God through its own wisdom. So God chose to use the message that sounds foolish to save those who believe. 22The Jews ask for miracles, and the Greeks want wisdom. 23But we preach a crucified Christ. This is a big problem to the Jews, and it is foolishness to those who are not Jews. 24But Christ is the power of God and the wisdom of God to those people God has called—Jews and Greeks. 25Even the foolishness of God is wiser than human wisdom, and the weakness of God is stronger than human strength.

26Brothers and sisters, look at what you were when God called you. Not many of you were wise in the way the world judges wisdom. Not many of you had great influence. Not many of you came from important families. 27But God chose the foolish things of the world to shame the wise, and he chose the weak things of the world to shame the strong. 28He chose what the world thinks is unimportant and what the world looks down on and thinks is nothing in order to destroy what the world thinks is important. 29God did this so that no one can brag in his presence. 30Because of God you are in Christ Jesus, who has become for us wisdom from God. In Christ we are put right with God, and have been made holy, and have been set free from sin. 31So, as the Scripture says, "If someone wants to brag, he should brag only about the Lord."

NKJV

18For the message of the cross is foolishness to those who are perishing, but to us who are being saved it is the power of God. 19For it is written:

"I will destroy the wisdom of the wise,

And bring to nothing the understanding of the prudent."

20Where is the wise? Where is the scribe? Where is the disputer of this age? Has not God made foolish the wisdom of this world? 21For since, in the wisdom of God, the world through wisdom did not know God, it pleased God through the foolishness of the message preached to save those who believe. 22For Jews request a sign, and Greeks seek after wisdom; 23but we preach Christ crucified, to the Jews a stumbling block and to the Greeks foolishness, 24but to those who are called, both Jews and Greeks, Christ the power of God and the wisdom of God. 25Because the foolishness of God is wiser than men, and the weakness of God is stronger than men.

²⁶*For you see your calling, brethren, that not many wise according to the flesh, not many mighty, not many noble, are called.* ²⁷*But God has chosen the foolish things of the world to put to shame the wise, and God has chosen the weak things of the world to put to shame the things which are mighty;* ²⁸*and the base things of the world and the things which are despised God has chosen, and the things which are not, to bring to nothing the things that are,* ²⁹*that no flesh should glory in His presence.* ³⁰*But of Him you are in Christ Jesus, who became for us wisdom from God—and righteousness and sanctification and redemption—*³¹*that, as it is written, "He who glories, let him glory in the Lord."*

EXPLORATION

1. In what ways can the gospel seem foolish? Have there been times in your life when all or part of the gospel seemed foolish to you? How?

2. How do Jesus' life and death reveal the wisdom and power of God?

3. In what ways is God's wisdom different from the world's wisdom?

4. What does Paul mean when he says God "chose the weak things of the world"?

5. So what do believers have to brag about? There's certainly a difference between talking about something or someone praiseworthy and talking about ourselves. There are different types of bragging. To which is Paul referring?

INSPIRATION

You want success? Here's your model. You want achievement? Here's your prototype. You want bright lights, pageants, and media attention? Consider the front-page, center article of the nation's largest daily newspaper. It is a caricature of "Miss America." The vital data of the fifty-one participants has been compiled to present the perfect woman. She has brown hair. She has brown eyes. She knows how to sing and has a perfect figure: 35–24–35. She is Miss America.

The message trumpets off the page: "This is the standard for American women." The implication is clear: Do what it takes to be like her. Firm your thighs. Deepen your cleavage. Pamper your hair. Improve your walk.

No reference is made to her convictions . . . to her honesty . . . to her faith . . . or to her God. But you are told her hip size.

In a small photo, four inches to the left, is another woman. Her face is thin. Her skin is wrinkled, almost leathery. No makeup . . . no blush . . . no lipstick. There is a faint smile on her lips and a glint in her eyes. She looks pale. Perhaps it's my imagination or perhaps it's time. The caption reads, "Mother Teresa: In serious condition."

Mother Teresa. You know her story. When she won the Nobel Peace Prize in 1985, she gave the two hundred thousand dollars to the poor of Calcutta. When a businessman bought her a new car, she sold it and gave the money to the under-privileged. She owns nothing. She owes nothing.

Two women: Miss America and Mother Teresa. One walks the boardwalk; the other walks the alley. Two voices. One promises crowns, flowers, and crowds. The other promises service, surrender, and joy.

Now I have nothing against beauty pageants (although I have my reservations about them). But I do have something against the lying voices that noise our world. You've heard them. They tell you to swap your integrity for a new sale. To barter your convictions for an easy deal. To exchange your devotion for a quick thrill.

They whisper. They woo. They taunt. They tantalize. They flirt. They flatter. "Go ahead, it's O.K." "Just wait until tomorrow." "Don't worry, no one will know." "How could anything that feels so right be so wrong?" . . .

For amidst the fleeting promises of pleasure is the timeless promise of [God's] presence.

"Surely I am with you always, to the very end of the age."

"Never will I leave you; never will I forsake you."

There is no chorus so loud that the voice of God cannot be heard . . . if we will but listen. (From *In the Eye of the Storm* by Max Lucado)

REACTION

6. In what ways do the media entice us to accept the world's values? Think of at least three or four forms of media and their effects.

7. In what situations have you sought God's guidance rather than relying on your own intellect and ability? Explain the circumstances and the outcome. Refer to Proverbs 3:5–7.

8. In what ways can we ignore the false messages around us and think more like God?

9. Why is it important to recognize the limits of human wisdom?

10. In what ways can you determine if an idea or plan is based on worldly thinking or biblical teaching?

11. List some benefits of living according to God's wisdom instead of human wisdom.

LIFE LESSONS

Two dangers immediately head the list when it comes to human wisdom: (1) it works (sometimes), and (2) it's mixed. Human wisdom seems effective. In a narrow way and for a while it may achieve success. People often do wrong and appear to get away with it. Human wisdom declares, "It's only wrong if you get caught." But the long-term, godly view of events demonstrates the failures of human wisdom. Unfortunately, life is often not long enough to learn the lesson. But human wisdom is also mixed. It borrows from true wisdom. What makes sense in human wisdom is often borrowed from God's wisdom. But the conclusions and applications are wrong. Human wisdom needs a truth grid, a test. One of the priceless roles of God's Word is the way it tests and corrects human wisdom.

DEVOTION

Father, too often the lies of the world drown out your voice. Give us ears to hear you and hearts willing to obey. Help us to stand against the pressure to seek success and power. Give us the strength to choose the timeless truths of your Word over the fleeting promises of the world. And Father, confirm only those thoughts and plans that conform to your will.

For more Bible passages on the limits of human wisdom, see Proverbs 3:5, 7; Ecclesiastes 1:12–18; 2:16; Jeremiah 9:23–24; Ezekiel 28:2–7; Matthew 11:25; 1 Corinthians 3:19–20.

To complete the book of 1 Corinthians during this twelve-part study, read 1 Corinthians 1:1–31.

JOURNALING

In light of this passage, how can I make better decisions?

LESSON TWO

GOD'S
WISDOM
REVEALED

MAX
LUCADO

REFLECTION

In the light of the last lesson, we've seen that we need to have discernment and not just follow the world's wisdom. What are your "tests" for discerning good advice? Think of someone who consistently gives you good advice. How has that person's wise counsel helped you in a specific situation?

SITUATION

The Corinthians were not only divided; they were also argumentative. Although the believers in Corinth came from humble backgrounds (1:26–29), some of them seemed eager to claim worldly wisdom for the faith rather than standing with Christ. Paul reminded them of his own behavior among them. His impact was not based on charismatic debates but a simple message of Christ. He called them back to their original point of faith.

OBSERVATION

Read 1 Corinthians 2:6–16 from the NCV or the NKJV.

NCV

⁶However, I speak a wisdom to those who are mature. But this wisdom is not from this world or from the rulers of this world, who are losing their power. ⁷I speak God's secret wisdom, which he has kept hidden. Before the world began, God planned this wisdom for our glory. ⁸None of the rulers of this world understood it. If they had, they would not have crucified the Lord of glory. ⁹But as it is written in the Scriptures:

"No one has ever seen this,

and no one has ever heard about it.

No one has ever imagined

what God has prepared for those who love him."

¹⁰But God has shown us these things through the Spirit.

The Spirit searches out all things, even the deep secrets of God. ¹¹Who knows the thoughts that another person has? Only a person's spirit that lives within him knows his thoughts. It is the same with God. No one knows the thoughts of God except the Spirit of God. ¹²Now we did not receive the spirit of the world, but we received the Spirit that is from God so that we can know all that God has given us. ¹³And we speak about these things, not with words taught us by human wisdom but with words taught us by the Spirit. And so we explain spiritual truths to spiritual people. ¹⁴A person who does not have the Spirit does not accept the truths that come from the Spirit of God. That person thinks they are foolish and cannot understand them, because they can only be judged to be true by the Spirit. ¹⁵The spiritual person is able to judge all things, but no one can judge him. The Scripture says:

¹⁶"Who has known the mind of the Lord?

Who has been able to teach him?"

But we have the mind of Christ.

NKJV

⁶However, we speak wisdom among those who are mature, yet not the wisdom of this age, nor of the rulers of this age, who are coming to nothing. ⁷But we speak the wisdom of God in a mystery, the hidden wisdom which God ordained before the ages for our glory, ⁸which none of the rulers of this age knew; for had they known, they would not have crucified the Lord of glory.

⁹But as it is written:

"Eye has not seen, nor ear heard,

Nor have entered into the heart of man

The things which God has prepared for those who love Him."

10But God has revealed them to us through His Spirit. For the Spirit searches all things, yes, the deep things of God. 11For what man knows the things of a man except the spirit of the man which is in him? Even so no one knows the things of God except the Spirit of God. 12Now we have received, not the spirit of the world, but the Spirit who is from God, that we might know the things that have been freely given to us by God.

13These things we also speak, not in words which man's wisdom teaches but which the Holy Spirit teaches, comparing spiritual things with spiritual. 14But the natural man does not receive the things of the Spirit of God, for they are foolishness to him; nor can he know them, because they are spiritually discerned. 15But he who is spiritual judges all things, yet he himself is rightly judged by no one. 16For "who has known the mind of the Lord that he may instruct Him?" But we have the mind of Christ.

EXPLORATION

1. Why does God keep some things hidden from us? How might knowing a lot more turn into danger for us?

2. In what ways can we know God's thoughts and plans?

3. List some ways the Holy Spirit helps believers. (See John 14:26; 15:26; 16:13–15; 1 John 2:27.)

4. How does Paul explain in this passage why a person without the Spirit is unable to understand spiritual truths?

5. Explain what it means to "have the mind of Christ." (See Romans 11:34 and Philippians 2:5 for help.)

INSPIRATION

Does God have an ego problem?

No, but we do. We are about as responsible with applause as I was with the cake I won in the first grade. In the grand finale of the musical chairs competition, guess who had a seat? And guess what the little red headed, freckle-faced boy won? A tender, moist coconut cake. And guess what the boy wanted to do that night in one sitting? Eat the whole thing! Not half of it. Not a piece of it. All of it! After all, I'd won it.

But you know what my folks did? They rationed the cake. They gave me only what I could handle. Knowing that today's binge is tomorrow's bellyache, they made sure I didn't get sick on my success.

God does the same. He takes the cake. He takes the credit, not because he needs it, but because he knows we can't handle it. We aren't content with a bite of adulation; we tend to swallow it all. It messes with our systems. The praise swells our heads and shrinks our brains, and pretty soon we start thinking we had something to do with our survival. Pretty soon we forget we were made out of dirt and rescued from sin.

Pretty soon we start praying like the fellow at the religious caucus: "God, I thank you that the world has people like me. The man on the corner needs welfare—I don't. The prostitute on the street has AIDS—I don't. The drunk at the bar needs alcohol—I don't. The gay caucus needs morality—I don't. I thank you that the world has people like me."

Fortunately, there was a man in the same meeting who had deflected all the applause. Too contrite even to look to the skies, he bowed and prayed, "God have mercy on me, a sinner. Like my brother on welfare, I'm dependent on grace. Like my sister with AIDS, I'm infected with mistakes. Like my friend who drinks, I need something to ease my pain. And as you love and give direction to the gay, grant some to me as well. Have mercy on me, a sinner."

After telling a story like that, Jesus said, "I tell you, when this man went home, he was right with God, but the Pharisee was not. All who make themselves great will be made humble, but all who make themselves humble will be made great" (Luke 18:14 NCV). (From *Traveling Light* by Max Lucado)

REACTION

6. In what different ways do we try to gain wisdom? Why do we want it?

7. What happens when we rely on human wisdom instead of God's wisdom?

8. When has the Holy Spirit helped you understand or apply God's Word?

9. What practical steps can we take to reduce the risk of making foolish decisions?

10. What sometimes keeps you from seeking God's help?

11. In what ways can you depend more on God's Spirit to help you make wise decisions?

LIFE LESSONS

The most difficult part of God's wisdom is that it usually requires us to do what we don't want to do and asks us not to do what we want to do. God's wisdom offends our wills more than our minds. Partly because of its eternal source, God's wisdom acts with a larger perspective in mind. And God's wisdom is always trustworthy. Just as I discovered my parents' wisdom in rationing out my cake, so God's will wisely gives us what we need and what is best.

DEVOTION

Father, your plans for us are perfect. Yet we often doubt your promises, assuming we can take better care of ourselves than our Creator. Forgive us for ignoring the truth in your Word. Tune our ears to your Spirit's voice, and teach us to follow your ways. May our lives testify to your great wisdom and power.

For more Bible passages on God's wisdom, see Psalm 111:10; Proverbs 2:6; Isaiah 11:2; Jeremiah 10:12; Ephesians 1:16–17; Colossians 2:3; 2 Timothy 3:15; James 1:5.

To complete the book of 1 Corinthians during this twelve-part study, read 1 Corinthians 2:1–3:8.

JOURNALING

In what situation today do I need God's wisdom?

WORK THAT LASTS

MAX LUCADO

REFLECTION

There are countless ways to spend our time. But are we working for that which will last? Think about how your life is enriched by people who give of their time in a way that benefits you. What are some of the desires and drives that motivate people to volunteer in the community or your church?

SITUATION

Part of the Corinthian divisiveness resulted in "fan clubs" for certain spiritual leaders. Some of them followed Apollos; some of them had loyalty only to Paul or to Peter. This appalled the apostle. They were missing the point entirely. Their allegiance needed to be firmly rooted in one place—in Christ alone. Paul pointed out the uselessness of any work done without that foundation.

OBSERVATION

Read from 1 Corinthians 3:9–15 from the NCV or the NKJV.

NCV

⁹*We are God's workers, working together; you are like God's farm, God's house.*

¹⁰*Using the gift God gave me, I laid the foundation of that house like an expert builder. Others are building on that foundation, but all people should be careful how they build on it. ¹¹The foundation that has already been laid is Jesus Christ, and no one can lay down any other foundation. ¹²But if people build on that foundation, using gold, silver, jewels, wood, grass, or straw, ¹³their work will be clearly seen, because the Day of Judgment will make it visible. That Day will appear with fire, and the fire will test everyone's work to show what sort of work it was. ¹⁴If the building that has been put on the foundation still stands, the builder will get a reward. ¹⁵But if the building is burned up, the builder will suffer loss. The builder will be saved, but it will be as one who escaped from a fire.*

NKJV

⁹*For we are God's fellow workers; you are God's field, you are God's building. ¹⁰According to the grace of God which was given to me, as a wise master builder I have laid the foundation, and another builds on it. But let each one take heed how he builds on it. ¹¹For no other foundation can anyone lay than that which is laid, which is Jesus Christ. ¹²Now if anyone builds on this foundation with gold, silver, precious stones, wood, hay, straw, ¹³each one's work will become clear; for the Day will declare it, because it will be revealed by fire; and the fire will test each one's work, of what sort it is. ¹⁴If anyone's work which he has built on it endures, he will receive a reward. ¹⁵If anyone's work is burned, he will suffer loss; but he himself will be saved, yet so as through fire.*

EXPLORATION

1. Jesus is the foundation of the church. What does that mean in today's world?

2. In what authentic and lasting ways can we build on the foundation that God has laid?

3. God will test the quality of our work as fire tests the quality of building materials. What kinds of work will withstand that test?

4. What are the rewards of building God's kingdom faithfully and with the best materials?

5. Work for God that is less than excellent is compared to a straw house that will burn up in the fire of judgment. What kind of behavior or service is like a straw house?

INSPIRATION

A large American food company released the perfect cake mix. It required no additives. No eggs, no sugar. Just mix some water with the powder, pop the pan in the oven, and presto! Prepare yourself for a treat.

One problem surfaced. No one purchased the product! Puzzled, the manufacturer conducted surveys, identified the reason, and reissued the cake with a slight alteration. The instructions now called for the cook to add one egg. Sales skyrocketed!

Why are we like that? What makes us want to add to what is already complete? Paul asked the same questions. People puzzled him by adding their work to a finished project. Not eggs to a recipe but requirements for salvation . . .

"God's way of making us right with himself depends on faith—counting on *Christ alone*" (Philippians 3:9 TLB, emphasis mine). Paul proclaimed a pure grace: no mixtures, no additives, no alterations. The work of Christ is the bungee cord for the soul. Trust it and take the plunge.

We quickly side with Paul on the circumcision controversy. The whole discussion sounds odd to our Western ears. But is it so strange? We may not teach Jesus + circumcision, but how about:

Jesus + evangelism: *How many people have you led to Christ this year?* Or:

Jesus + contributions: *Are you giving all you can to the church?* Or:

Jesus + mysticism: *You do offer penance and pray to the Virgin Mary, don't you?* Or:

Jesus + heritage: *Were you raised in "the church"?* Or:

Jesus + doctrine: *When you were baptized, was the water running or still? Deep or shallow? Hot or cold?*

Legalism. The theology of "Jesus + . . . " Legalists don't dismiss Christ. They trust in Christ a lot. But they don't trust in Christ alone. (From *It's Not About Me* by Max Lucado)

REACTION

6. What should be the driving force behind our work for God?

7. Why is it tempting to evaluate our success according to external results? What happens when we give in to that temptation?

8. Describe what kind of work counts for eternity.

9. What obstacles keep us from getting more involved in ministry?

10. In what ways can we evaluate the quality of our service?

11. List some practical ways you can invest yourself in God's kingdom.

LIFE LESSONS

Healthy Christian mentor relationships can easily take a wrong turn. We need to learn from believers who are more experienced than we are, but we make a mistake if our faith begins to rest more on our teacher than on Christ. Trustworthy leaders always point to Christ, not themselves. They expect us to follow them only so long as they are clearly following Christ. The work we do for Christ must never be seen as an added part of the foundation that rests on Jesus alone. Gold flows from gratitude-based actions toward Christ. Any other motivation tends to produce wood, hay, and stubble.

DEVOTION

Father, thank you for laying the perfect foundation for your church. Now show us how to build on that foundation. Give us a burning desire to build your church. Help us to see what is important and what is lasting. Let us make decisions based on eternity and not on temporary possessions. Most of all, Father, help us to seek your kingdom and your righteousness.

For more Bible passages on work that lasts, see Luke 12:33; John 6:27; 2 Corinthians 4:17–18; Colossians 3:23–24; Hebrews 10:34–35.

To complete the book of 1 Corinthians during this twelve-part study, read 1 Corinthians 3:9–23.

JOURNALING

What is my role in building God's church?

LESSON FOUR

SERVING
CHRIST

MAX
LUCADO

REFLECTION

Think of someone who has served Christ for many years. Consider the ways that person's example has inspired you. Identify some of the traits that person has that you want to develop in your own life.

SITUATION

Groups within the Corinthian church were not only aligning themselves with the names of leaders such as Paul and Apollos, but they were also developing an attitude of independence and pride. They were using recognizable names but practicing their own brand of spirituality. Paul had to confront their selective and comfortable spiritual lives.

OBSERVATION

Read 1 Corinthians 4:6–19 from the NCV or the NKJV.

NCV

6Brothers and sisters, I have used Apollos and myself as examples so you could learn through us the meaning of the saying, "Follow only what is written in the Scriptures." Then you will not be more proud of one person than another. 7Who says you are better than others? What do you have that was not given to you? And if it was given to you, why do you brag as if you did not receive it as a gift?

8You think you already have everything you need. You think you are rich. You think you have become kings without us. I wish you really were kings so we could be kings together with you. 9But it seems to me that God has put us apostles in last place, like those sentenced to die. We are like a show for the whole world to see—angels and people. 10We are fools for Christ's sake, but you are very wise in Christ. We are weak, but you are strong. You receive honor, but we are shamed. 11Even to this very hour we do not have enough to eat or drink or to wear. We are often beaten, and we have no homes in which to live. 12We work hard with our own hands for our food. When people curse us, we bless them. When they hurt us, we put up with it. 13When they tell evil lies about us, we speak nice words about them. Even today, we are treated as though we were the garbage of the world—the filth of the earth.

14I am not trying to make you feel ashamed. I am writing this to give you a warning as my own dear children. 15For though you may have ten thousand teachers in Christ, you do not have many fathers. Through the Good News I became your father in Christ Jesus, 16so I beg you, please follow my example. 17That is why I am sending to you Timothy, my son in the Lord. I love Timothy, and he is faithful. He will help you remember my way of life in Christ Jesus, just as I teach it in all the churches everywhere.

18Some of you have become proud, thinking that I will not come to you again. 19But I will come to you very soon if the Lord wishes. Then I will know what the proud ones do, not what they say.

NKJV

6Now these things, brethren, I have figuratively transferred to myself and Apollos for your sakes, that you may learn in us not to think beyond what is written, that none of you may be puffed up on behalf of one against the other. 7For who makes you differ from another? And what do you have that you did not receive? Now if you did indeed receive it, why do you boast as if you had not received it?

[8]*You are already full! You are already rich! You have reigned as kings without us—and indeed I could wish you did reign, that we also might reign with you!* [9]*For I think that God has displayed us, the apostles, last, as men condemned to death; for we have been made a spectacle to the world, both to angels and to men.* [10]*We are fools for Christ's sake, but you are wise in Christ! We are weak, but you are strong! You are distinguished, but we are dishonored!* [11]*To the present hour we both hunger and thirst, and we are poorly clothed, and beaten, and homeless.* [12]*And we labor, working with our own hands. Being reviled, we bless; being persecuted, we endure;* [13]*being defamed, we entreat. We have been made as the filth of the world, the offscouring of all things until now.*

[14]*I do not write these things to shame you, but as my beloved children I warn you.* [15]*For though you might have ten thousand instructors in Christ, yet you do not have many fathers; for in Christ Jesus I have begotten you through the gospel.* [16]*Therefore I urge you, imitate me.* [17]*For this reason I have sent Timothy to you, who is my beloved and faithful son in the Lord, who will remind you of my ways in Christ, as I teach everywhere in every church.*

[18]*Now some are puffed up, as though I were not coming to you.* [19]*But I will come to you shortly, if the Lord wills, and I will know, not the word of those who are puffed up, but the power.*

EXPLORATION

1. Paul saw evidence of spiritual pride in the early church. Why did that trouble him? (Think of the term "spiritual pride" as referring to one Christian judging whether a fellow Christian is a good follower of Christ. Often that results in arrogance. Evaluating others tempts us with the attitude that we are better than they are.)

2. Our abilities and talents are gifts from God. As we identify them and begin to use them, what will keep us from thinking that we are better than others?

3. Is there anything wrong with taking the credit for our accomplishments?

4. Paul believed apostles should stand in last place. What does that tell us about Paul's attitude toward status and position (particularly compared to how we weigh status and position today)?

5. What should we be willing to give up to serve Christ?

INSPIRATION

The scene is almost spooky: a tall, unfinished tower looming solitarily on a dusty plain. Its base is wide and strong but covered with weeds. Large stones originally intended for use in the tower lie forsaken on the ground. Buckets, hammers, and pulleys—all lie abandoned. The silhouette cast by the structure is lean and lonely.

Not too long ago, this tower was buzzing with activity. A bystander would have been impressed with the smooth-running construction of the world's first sky-scraper. One group of workers stirred freshly made mortar. Another team pulled bricks out of the oven. A third group carried the bricks to the construction site while a fourth shouldered the load up a winding path to the top of the tower where it was firmly set in place.

Their dream was a tower. A tower that would be taller than anyone had ever dreamed. A tower that would punch through the clouds and scratch the heavens. And what was the purpose of the tower? To glorify God? No. To try to find God? No. To call people to look upward to God? Try again. To provide a heavenly haven of prayer? Still wrong.

The purpose of the work caused its eventual abortion. The method was right. The plan was effective. But the motive was wrong. Dead wrong. Read these minutes from the "Tower Planning Committee Meeting" and see what I mean:

"Come, let us build ourselves a city, and a tower with its top in the heavens, and [watch out] let us make a name for ourselves."

Why was the tower being built? Selfishness. Pure, 100-percent selfishness. The bricks were made of inflated egos and the mortar was made of pride. Men were giving sweat and blood for a pillar. Why? So that somebody's name could be remembered.

We have a name for that: blind ambition.

We make heroes out of people who are ambitious.

And rightly so. This world would be in sad shape without people who dream of touching the heavens. Ambition is that grit in the soul which creates disenchantment with the ordinary and puts the dare into dreams.

But left unchecked it becomes an insatiable addition to power and prestige; a roaring hunger for achievement that devours people as a lion devours an animal, leaving behind only the skeletal remains of relationships.

Blind ambition. Distorted values.

God won't tolerate it. He didn't then and he won't now. He took the "Climb to Heaven Campaign" into his hands. With one sweep he painted the tower gray with confusion and sent workers babbling in all directions. He took man's greatest achievement and blew it into the winds like a child blows a dandelion.

Are you building any towers? Examine your motives. And remember the statement imprinted on the base of the windswept Tower of Babel: Blind ambition is a giant step away from God and one step closer to catastrophe. (From *God Came Near* by Max Lucado)

REACTION

6. What is the potential danger in trying to achieve great things for God?

7. What are some ways selfish ambition can create problems in the church?

8. How can we determine whether our service to God is Christ-centered or self-centered? What examples would you use to illustrate this principle?

9. In what ways can we curb our appetite for prestige and power? What do we have to watch for in our relational and spiritual "diet"?

10. When God gives us success in ministry, how can we guard against pride?

11. How can we give God appropriate credit for the things he has accomplished through us?

LIFE LESSONS

Refusing to take credit for our part in something good doesn't necessarily indicate a lack of pride. And taking credit for our contribution doesn't necessarily indicate pride. Paul admitted that he was the "father" of the Corinthian church. That wasn't pride; it was a statement of fact used to anchor a significant lesson. Paul's counsel to the Roman believers ought to be our constant guide: "For I say, through the grace given to me, to everyone who is among you, not to think of himself more highly than he ought to think, but to think soberly, as God has dealt to each one a measure of faith" (Rom. 12:3 NKJV). Spiritual pride is a persistent pit that lies alongside a believer's pathway. We are in greatest danger of stumbling into that void in the moments after we think we have just done something humble.

DEVOTION

O Father, forgive us for our arrogance, for acting as though we can accomplish great things on our own. We are nothing without you. Teach us to recognize our complete dependence on you and to surrender our desires and ambitions. Make our service more pleasing in your sight.

For more Bible passages on serving Christ, see Matthew 20:25–28; John 12:25–26; Romans 12:10–11; 14:17–18; Ephesians 6:7.

To complete the book of 1 Corinthians during this twelve-part study, read 1 Corinthians 4:1–6:20.

JOURNALING

What personal goals or desires do I need to reevaluate in light of this passage?

LESSON FIVE

SELF-
SACRIFICE

MAX
LUCADO

REFLECTION

Of all the creatures that live on the earth, human beings are among the least self-sufficient. Newborn animals can often survive in hostile environments, but we are born almost completely dependent on the sacrifice of others for our survival. We arrive naked and desperately in need of covering that someone else must provide. In the same way, the sacrifices of others are necessary in encouraging our spiritual growth after we are born again. Our spiritual lives are not intended to be self-centered, but we are to live lives of sacrificial love. Describe a time when someone sacrificed his or her own needs to help you.

SITUATION

In his letter Paul has responded to specific questions from the Corinthian believers. The divisiveness and self-centeredness (posing as freedom) in the church has created chaos in the practices and lives of believers. Paul is maintaining the truth of the wonderful freedom in Christ, while warning Christians that an overemphasis on freedom (rather than on Christ) quickly leads to bondage and conflict. Freedom, Paul writes, must be balanced with self-sacrifice for Christ's sake.

OBSERVATION

Read 1 Corinthians 9:16–22 from the NCV or the NKJV.

NCV

¹⁶Telling the Good News does not give me any reason for bragging. Telling the Good News is my duty—something I must do. And how terrible it will be for me if I do not tell the Good News. ¹⁷If I preach because it is my own choice, I have a reward. But if I preach and it is not my choice to do so, I am only doing the duty that was given to me. ¹⁸So what reward do I get? This is my reward: that when I tell the Good News I can offer it freely. I do not use my full rights in my work of preaching the Good News.

¹⁹I am free and belong to no one. But I make myself a slave to all people to win as many as I can. ²⁰To the Jews I became like a Jew to win the Jews. I myself am not ruled by the law. But to those who are ruled by the law I became like a person who is ruled by the law. I did this to win those who are ruled by the law. ²¹To those who are without the law I became like a person who is without the law. I did this to win those people who are without the law. (But really, I am not without God's law—I am ruled by Christ's law.) ²²To those who are weak, I became weak so I could win the weak. I have become all things to all people so I could save some of them in any way possible.

NKJV

¹⁶For if I preach the gospel, I have nothing to boast of, for necessity is laid upon me; yes, woe is me if I do not preach the gospel! ¹⁷For if I do this willingly, I have a reward; but if against my will, I have been entrusted with a stewardship. ¹⁸What is my reward then? That when I preach the gospel, I may present the gospel of Christ without charge, that I may not abuse my authority in the gospel.

¹⁹For though I am free from all men, I have made myself a servant to all, that I might win the more; ²⁰and to the Jews I became as a Jew, that I might win Jews; to those who are under the law, as under the law, that I might win those who are under the law; ²¹to those who are without law, as without law (not being without law toward God, but under law toward Christ), that I might win those who are without law; ²²to the weak I became as weak, that I might win the weak. I have become all things to all men, that I might by all means save some.

EXPLORATION

1. Paul gave up some of his rights to preach the Good News. Why did he do that?

2. Explain what it means to become a "slave to all people." What kind of language could we use today to get the same point across?

3. Paul was not as concerned with his method of evangelism as with the message he was proclaiming. How can we apply his thinking to our evangelism today?

4. Think about the times you try to be a witness for Christ. What have you learned in those experiences that you can share with others?

5. What behaviors, attitudes, or beliefs can hinder our Christian witness?

INSPIRATION

We are much like Ruth and Verena Cady. Since their birth in 1984 they have shared much. Just like twins, they have shared a bike, a bed, a room, and toys. They've shared meals and stories and TV shows and birthdays. They shared the same womb before they were born and the same room after they were born. But the bond between Ruthie and Verena goes even further. They share more than toys and treats; they share the same heart.

Their bodies are fused together from the sternum to the waist. Though they have separate nervous systems and distinct personalities, they are sustained by the same, singular three-chambered heart. Neither could survive without the other. Since separation is not an option, cooperation becomes an obligation.

They have learned to work together. Take walking, for example. Their mother assumed they would take turns walking forward or backwards. It made sense to her that they would alternate; one facing the front and the other the back. The girls had a better idea. They learned to walk sideways, almost like dancing. And they dance in the same direction . . .

When one has to sit in the corner, so does the other. The innocent party doesn't complain; both learned early that they are stuck together for the good and the bad. Which is just one of the many lessons these girls can teach those of us who live in God's Great House.

Don't we share the same kitchen? Aren't we covered by the same roof and protected by the same walls? We don't sleep in the same bed, but we sleep under the same sky. We aren't sharing one heart . . . but then again maybe we are; for don't we share the same hope for eternity, the same hurt from rejection, and the same hunger to be loved? Like the Cady twins, don't we have the same Father?

We don't pray to *my* Father or ask for *my* daily bread or ask God to forgive *my* sins. In God's house we speak the language of plurality; "*our* Father," "*our* daily bread," "*our* debts," "*our* debtors," "lead *us* not into temptation," and "deliver *us* . . ."

From God's perspective we have much in common. Jesus lists these common denominators in his prayer. They are easy to find. Every time we see the word *our* or *us*, we find a need. (From *The Great House of God* by Max Lucado)

REACTION

6. In this lesson's Bible passage, Paul said he gave up his own rights, preferences, and styles in order to share the gospel. How does this contradict human nature?

7. Why is it so difficult for us to give up our rights? What are some of the ones we struggle over in the church?

8. List some of the benefits of self-sacrifice. (For help in compiling this list, see Matthew 19:21 and Luke 14:26.)

9. Explain how a spirit of humility contributes to effective witnessing.

10. How can we combat our natural tendency to fight for our rights?

11. List some ways you can cultivate a spirit of humility.

LIFE LESSONS

Like love, humility has less to do with feelings than it has to do with decisions, motivations, and actions. Humility as a feeling is probably similar to nitro-glycerin—shake it and it blows up. But God's Word gives us numerous guidelines and challenges to live humbly. In a world that boldly encourages us to think about ourselves first, the discipline of humility chooses to focus on others. So often our real needs are met as we seek to meet the needs of others.

Self-sacrifice doesn't look like fun, feel like fun, or seem like fun. But then fun isn't the final goal, is it? The greatest example of self-sacrifice wasn't carried out because it was fun; it was carried out because of the ultimate joy that would result. "Looking unto Jesus, the author and finisher of our faith, who for the joy that was set before Him endured the cross, despising the shame, and has sat down at the right hand of the throne of God" (Heb. 12:2 NKJV).

DEVOTION

Father, long before we repented or even acknowledged our need for you, you sent your only Son to die for our sins. What amazing love! O Father, help us to be more like you. Fill us with your love, so that we will gladly sacrifice everything to win more souls for you. Take our eyes off ourselves, our rights and desires. May we extend your hand of grace and mercy to the lost.

For more Bible passages on self-sacrifice, see Romans 12:1–2; Philippians 2:3–5; Hebrews 13:16; 1 Peter 2:5.

To complete the book of 1 Corinthians during this twelve-part study, read 1 Corinthians 7:1–9:27.

JOURNALING

What am I willing to give up to win more people to Christ?

LESSON SIX

TEMPTATION

MAX LUCADO

REFLECTION

Days without temptation of one kind or another are rare. Having a personal strategy to handle temptation remains a central component to healthy spiritual growth. Think of a time when you felt tempted by something. How did God help you?

SITUATION

Stepping back from the specific questions and issues he has been addressing, Paul sketches the big picture of God's operations in the world. He draws attention to the negative events and positive lessons that fill the Old Testament and their usefulness in our lives.

OBSERVATION

Read 1 Corinthians 10:1–13 from the NCV or the NKJV.

NCV

¹Brothers and sisters, I want you to know what happened to our ancestors who followed Moses. They were all under the cloud and all went through the sea. ²They were all baptized as followers of Moses in the cloud and in the sea. ³They all ate the same spiritual food, ⁴and all drank the same spiritual drink. They drank from that spiritual rock that followed them, and that rock was Christ. ⁵But God was not pleased with most of them, so they died in the desert.

⁶And these things happened as examples for us, to stop us from wanting evil things as those people did. ⁷Do not worship idols, as some of them did. Just as it is written in the Scriptures: "They sat down to eat and drink, and then they got up and sinned sexually." ⁸We must not take part in sexual sins, as some of them did. In one day twenty-three thousand of them died because of their sins. ⁹We must not test Christ as some of them did; they were killed by snakes. ¹⁰Do not complain as some of them did; they were killed by the angel that destroys.

¹¹The things that happened to those people are examples. They were written down to teach us, because we live in a time when all these things of the past have reached their goal. ¹²If you think you are strong, you should be careful not to fall. ¹³The only temptation that has come to you is that which everyone has. But you can trust God, who will not permit you to be tempted more than you can stand. But when you are tempted, he will also give you a way to escape so that you will be able to stand it.

NKJV

¹Moreover, brethren, I do not want you to be unaware that all our fathers were under the cloud, all passed through the sea, ²all were baptized into Moses in the cloud and in the sea, ³all ate the same spiritual food, ⁴and all drank the same spiritual drink. For they drank of that spiritual Rock that followed them, and that Rock was Christ. ⁵But with most of them God was not well pleased, for their bodies were scattered in the wilderness.

⁶Now these things became our examples, to the intent that we should not lust after evil things as they also lusted. ⁷And do not become idolaters as were some of them. As it is written, "The people sat down to eat and drink, and rose up to play." ⁸Nor let us commit sexual immorality, as some of them did, and in one day twenty-three thousand fell; ⁹nor let us tempt Christ, as some of them also tempted, and were destroyed by serpents; ¹⁰nor complain, as some of them also complained, and were destroyed by the destroyer. ¹¹Now all these things happened to them as examples, and they were written for our admonition, upon whom the ends of the ages have come.

¹²Therefore let him who thinks he stands take heed lest he fall. ¹³No temptation has overtaken you except such as is common to man; but God is faithful, who will not allow you to be tempted beyond what you are able, but with the temptation will also make the way of escape, that you may be able to bear it.

EXPLORATION

1. How is Israel's history relevant to us today?

2. What are some consequences of giving in to temptation over and over again? (For Old Testament details, see Numbers 14.)

3. What does this passage reveal about the difference between human nature and God's character?

4. What encouragement does Scripture offer us about how to face temptation?

5. List some of the ways God helps us resist sin.

INSPIRATION

Real change is an inside job. You might alter things a day or two with money and systems, but the heart of the matter is, and always will be, the matter of the heart.

Allow me to get specific. Our problem is sin. Not finances. Not budgets. Not overcrowded prisons or drug dealers. Our problem is sin. We are in rebellion against our Creator. We are separated from our Father. We are cut off from the source of life. A new president or policy won't fix that. It can only be solved by God.

That's why the Bible uses drastic terms like *conversion, repentance,* and *lost,* and *found.* Society may renovate, but only God re-creates.

Here is a practical exercise to put this truth into practice. The next time alarms go off in your world, ask yourself three questions:

Is there any unconfessed sin in my life?

Are there any unresolved conflicts in my world?

Are there any unsurrendered worries in my heart?

Alarms serve a purpose. They signal a problem. Sometimes the problem is out there. More often it's in here. So before you peek outside, take a good look inside. (From *When God Whispers Your Name* by Max Lucado)

REACTION

6. List some of the warning signs God uses to help us say no to sin.

7. Why do we sometimes ignore the warning signs God provides?

8. Think about a time when you gave in to temptation. What might have helped you be stronger?

9. Why is it important for us to understand our inclination toward sin?

10. How does consistent time in God's Word fortify us in our areas of weakness?

11. What do you plan to do differently the next time you are tempted?

LIFE LESSONS

This passage in 1 Corinthians represents one of the classic examples of "life lessons" in Scripture. The events in the Bible were recorded for us as examples and admonitions. We can learn from our reading and be warned by the experiences of others. Even when we are confident that we are on track in our spiritual lives, we must "take heed lest we fall." Our attentiveness can take two forms: first, a continual effort to avoid sin, and second, a willingness to count on God's help when we face temptation.

DEVOTION

Father, your Word says that no temptation will be too strong for us to bear and that you will always show us a way to resist sin. We claim your promises and ask you to give us the strength to use the escape routes you provide. And we pray that in our hours of desperation and weakness, you would help us feel your presence.

For more Bible passages on temptation, see Matthew 4:1–11; 26:41; Luke 11:4; Galatians 6:1; 1 Thessalonians 3:5; 1 Timothy 6:9; Hebrews 2:17–18; 4:15–16; James 1:13–15.

To complete the book of 1 Corinthians during this twelve-part study, read 1 Corinthians 10:1–13.

JOURNALING

What keeps me from taking the escape routes that God provides?

LIBERTY AND LOVE

MAX LUCADO

REFLECTION

Think for a few moments about what freedom means to you. What new freedoms have you enjoyed since you became a Christian? In what ways do you think your freedom in Christ is different from any other freedom you may have experienced?

SITUATION

Some of the believers in Corinth were taking their freedom in Christ to offensive extremes. Like the Romans Paul addressed in Romans 6, they were in danger of using grace as an excuse to sin. If the exercise of spiritual freedom means that others are harmed, then that exercise of freedom has to be reevaluated. Paul saw numerous instances in the Corinthians' lives where this principle could be applied.

OBSERVATION

Read 1 Corinthians 10:23–33 from the NCV or the NKJV. ·

NCV

²³"We are allowed to do all things," but all things are not good for us to do. "We are allowed to do all things," but not all things help others grow stronger. ²⁴Do not look out only for yourselves. Look out for the good of others also.

²⁵Eat any meat that is sold in the meat market. Do not ask questions to see if it is meat you think is wrong to eat. ²⁶You may eat it, "because the earth belongs to the Lord, and everything in it."

²⁷Those who are not believers may invite you to eat with them. If you want to go, eat anything that is put before you. Do not ask questions to see if you think it might be wrong to eat. ²⁸But if anyone says to you, "That food was offered to idols," do not eat it. Do not eat it because of that person who told you and because eating it might be thought to be wrong. ²⁹I don't mean you think it is wrong, but the other person might. But why, you ask, should my freedom be judged by someone else's conscience? ³⁰If I eat the meal with thankfulness, why am I criticized because of something for which I thank God?

³¹The answer is, if you eat or drink, or if you do anything, do it all for the glory of God. ³²Never do anything that might hurt others—Jews, Greeks, or God's church—³³just as I, also, try to please everybody in every way. I am not trying to do what is good for me but what is good for most people so they can be saved.

NKJV

²³All things are lawful for me, but not all things are helpful; all things are lawful for me, but not all things edify. ²⁴Let no one seek his own, but each one the other's well-being.

²⁵Eat whatever is sold in the meat market, asking no questions for conscience' sake; ²⁶for "the earth is the Lord's, and all its fullness."

²⁷If any of those who do not believe invites you to dinner, and you desire to go, eat whatever is set before you, asking no question for conscience' sake. ²⁸But if anyone says to you, "This was offered to idols," do not eat it for the sake of the one who told you, and for conscience' sake; for "the earth is the Lord's, and all its fullness." ²⁹"Conscience," I say, not your own, but that of the other. For why is my liberty judged by another man's conscience? ³⁰But if I partake with thanks, why am I evil spoken of for the food over which I give thanks?

³¹Therefore, whether you eat or drink, or whatever you do, do all to the glory of God. ³²Give no offense, either to the Jews or to the Greeks or to the church of God, ³³just as I also please all men in all things, not seeking my own profit, but the profit of many, that they may be saved.

EXPLORATION

1. What limits our Christian freedom? *not to offend others*

2. Explain the relationship between our freedom to enjoy all of life and our limitations out of love for our sisters and brothers in Christ.

3. What should Christians consider when making ethical decisions?
the effect on others

4. What is meant by causing our weaker brothers and sisters to stumble in their faith?

Be considerate

5. What should be our primary concern in making lifestyle choices?

to honor God, not to offend.

INSPIRATION

Life is tough enough as it is. It's even tougher when we're headed in the wrong direction.

One of the incredible abilities of Jesus was to stay on target. His life never got off track. Not once do we find him walking down the wrong side of the fairway. He had no money, no computers, no jets, no administrative assistants or staff, yet Jesus did what many of us fail to do. He kept his life on course.

As Jesus looked across the horizon of his future, he could see many targets. Many flags were flapping in the wind, each of which he could have pursued. He could have been a political revolutionary. He could have been a national leader. He could have been content to be a teacher and educate minds or to be a physician and heal bodies. But in the end he chose to be a Savior and save souls.

Anyone near Christ for any length of time heard it from Jesus himself. "The Son of Man came to find lost people and save them" (Luke 19:10 NCV). "The Son of Man did not come to be served. He came to serve others and to give his life as a ransom for many people" (Mark 10:45 NCV).

The heart of Christ was relentlessly focused on one task. The day he left the carpentry shop of Nazareth he had one ultimate aim: the cross of Calvary. He was so focused that his final words were, "It is finished" (John 19:30 NCV).

How could Jesus say he was finished? There were still the hungry to feed, the sick to heal, the untaught to instruct, and the unloved ones to love. How could he say he was finished? Simple. He had completed his designated task. His commission was fulfilled. The painter could set aside the brush, the sculptor lay down his chisel, the writer put away his pen. The job was done.

Wouldn't you love to be able to say the same? Wouldn't you love to look back on your life and know you had done what you were called to do?

Our lives tend to be so scattered. We're intrigued by one trend only until the next comes along. Suckers for the latest craze or quick fix. This project, then another. Lives with no strategy, no goal, no defining priority. Playing holes out of order. Erratic. Hesitant. Living life with the hiccups. We are easily distracted by the small things and forget the big things . . . God wants us to be just like Jesus and have focused lives. (From *Just Like Jesus* by Max Lucado)

REACTION

6. What does it mean to express our liberty wisely? Based on the Lucado quote you just read, how did Jesus exercise his freedom?

Being focused —

7. Explain the difference between tolerating differences and condoning wrong behavior. Choose your examples carefully. *Carefully !*

8. Why is it crucial for believers to love and accept one another? How did Jesus model the approach he expects us to imitate? *patience*

9. What characteristics of the world would be different if all Christians lived according to the guidelines in this lesson's Bible passage?

10. How can arguments over controversial issues harm the church?

11. Think of one person to whom you can show greater sensitivity and love. List some examples of how you can do that.

LIFE LESSONS

Our freedom is always defined by Christ. Since he gave it to us as a gift, he's the best person to tell us how to use it. He may ask us to use it in ways that surprise us. Those actions may not seem like freedom when they involve saying no to our desires and saying yes to Christ's will for us. Some of our greatest moments of freedom come when we choose not to exercise our freedom in order to help someone else.

DEVOTION

Father, help us realize that you have truly set us free—free from the lures of status and materialism and peer pressure. Remind us that when the Son sets us free, we are free indeed. And Father, show us when to sacrifice our rights out of love for one another. Fill us with your Spirit so that our actions build up the church and bring glory to your name.

For more Bible passages on Christian freedom, see John 8:31–36; Romans 8:2; Galatians 4:4–5; 5:1–15; 1 Peter 2:16.

To complete the book of 1 Corinthians during this twelve-part study, read 1 Corinthians 10:14–11:34.

JOURNALING

In what ways can I find the balance between enjoying my freedom in Christ and giving up my rights to help others?

SPIRITUAL GIFTS

MAX LUCADO

LIFE LESSONS WITH MAX LUCADO

REFLECTION

Think of a role or responsibility you enjoy fulfilling in the church. Consider some
of the responsibilities others have accepted that benefit you spiritually. Think
about the accompanying feelings you have when you are doing for others what you
realize God has equipped you to do. Do you think these are just talents, or is there
some more intimate design at work in the body of Christ? Why do you think so?

SITUATION

Beginning with chapter 11, Paul confronts a central problem in Corinth. Their
corporate practice of worship has become distorted, chaotic, and dishonoring
to God. The church is so splintered that it can't function as a whole in worship.
Attitudes reflected in the way the members of the congregation dress, and particularly the way they celebrate the Lord's Supper, betray deep dysfunctions. The
spiritual distinctives (individual gifts) that should be a point of strength in the
church have become a point of weakness, confusion, and competition. Paul seeks
to step back and show his readers the big picture of God's gifts.

OBSERVATION

Read 1 Corinthians 12:1–11 from the NCV or the NKJV.

NCV

¹Now, brothers and sisters, I want you to understand about spiritual gifts. ²You know the way you lived before you were believers. You let yourselves be influenced and led away to worship idols—things that could not speak. ³So I want you to understand that no one who is speaking with the help of God's Spirit says, "Jesus be cursed." And no one can say, "Jesus is Lord," without the help of the Holy Spirit.

⁴There are different kinds of gifts, but they are all from the same Spirit. ⁵There are different ways to serve but the same Lord to serve. ⁶And there are different ways that God works through people but the same God. God works in all of us in everything we do. ⁷Something from the Spirit can be seen in each person, for the common good. ⁸The Spirit gives one person the ability to speak with wisdom, and the same Spirit gives another the ability to speak with knowledge. ⁹The same Spirit gives faith to one person. And, to another, that one Spirit gives gifts of healing. ¹⁰The Spirit gives to another person the power to do miracles, to another the ability to prophesy. And he gives to another the ability to know the difference between good and evil spirits. The Spirit gives one person the ability to speak in different kinds of languages and to another the ability to interpret those languages. ¹¹One Spirit, the same Spirit, does all these things, and the Spirit decides what to give each person.

NKJV

¹Now concerning spiritual gifts, brethren, I do not want you to be ignorant:² You know that you were Gentiles, carried away to these dumb idols, however you were led. ³Therefore I make known to you that no one speaking by the Spirit of God calls Jesus accursed, and no one can say that Jesus is Lord except by the Holy Spirit.

⁴There are diversities of gifts, but the same Spirit. ⁵There are differences of ministries, but the same Lord. ⁶And there are diversities of activities, but it is the same God who works all in all. ⁷But the manifestation of the Spirit is given to each one for the profit of all: ⁸for to one is given the word of wisdom through the Spirit, to another the word of knowledge through the same Spirit, ⁹to another faith by the same Spirit, to another gifts of healings by the same Spirit, ¹⁰to another the working of miracles, to another prophecy, to another discerning of spirits, to another different kinds of tongues, to another the interpretation of tongues. ¹¹But one and the same Spirit works all these things, distributing to each one individually as He wills.

EXPLORATION

1. The Holy Spirit distributes spiritual gifts to all believers. According to this passage, why is there such a variety of gifts?

2. What is the ultimate purpose of our spiritual gifts? What are some spiritual by-products that come from the exercise of gifts?

3. Though there are different gifts, there is only one God. Why is that important for us to remember? (For other Scriptures on gifts, see Romans 12:3–8 and Ephesians 4:1–13.)

4. What is our responsibility in regard to our spiritual gifts?

5. This passage says the Spirit gives a gift to everyone. Then why are there people who feel they have nothing to offer to their church? Which spiritual gifts might be helping other believers identify their gifts?

INSPIRATION

A few nights ago a peculiar thing happened.

An electrical storm caused a blackout in our neighborhood. When the lights went out, I felt my way through the darkness into the storage closet where we keep the candles for nights like this . . . I took my match and lit four of them. . . .

I was turning to leave with the large candle in my hand when I heard a voice, "Now, hold it right there."

"Who said that?"

"I did." The voice was near my hand.

"Who are you? What are you?"

"I'm a candle."

I lifted up the candle to take a closer look. You won't believe what I saw. There was a tiny face in the wax . . . a moving, functioning, fleshlike face full of expression and life.

"Don't take me out of here!"

"What?"

"I said, Don't take me out of this room."

"What do you mean? I have to take you out. You're a candle. Your job is to give light. It's dark out there."

"But you can't take me out. I'm not ready," the candle explained with pleading eyes. "I need more preparation."

I couldn't believe my ears. "More preparation?"

"Yeah, I've decided I need to research this job of light-giving so I won't go out and make a bunch of mistakes. You'd be surprised how distorted the glow of an untrained candle can be . . . "

"All right then, "I said. "You're not the only candle on the shelf. I'll blow you out and take the others!"

But just as I got my cheeks full of air, I heard other voices.

"We aren't going either!"

I turned around and looked at the three other candles . . . "You are candles and your job is to light dark places!"

"Well, that may be what you think," said the candle on the far left . . . "You may think we have to go, but I'm busy . . . I'm meditating on the importance of light. It's really enlightening."

"And you other two," I asked, "are you going to stay in here as well?"

A short, fat, purple candle with plump cheeks that reminded me of Santa Claus spoke up. "I'm waiting to get my life together. I'm not stable enough."

The last candle had a female voice, very pleasant to the ear. "I'd like to help," she explained, "but lighting the darkness is not my gift . . . I'm a singer. I sing to other candles to encourage them to burn more brightly."

She began a rendition of "This Little Light of Mine." The other three joined in, filling the storage room with singing . . . I took a step back and considered the absurdity of it all. Four perfectly healthy candles singing to each other about light but refusing to come out of the closet. (From *God Came Near* by Max Lucado)

REACTION

6. What prevents us from using our gifts? What explanations or excuses have you heard people use (or used yourself) about not using their gifts?

timid, fear.

7. In what ways can we all help one another identify our spiritual gifts?

By others, real talent

8. What is one thing you could do this week to share your gifts?

help others

9. What is wrong with saying that some gifts are superior to others?

1 Col 4 - 8 - 4

10. How can we use our gifts in a way that draws attention away from ourselves and gives the glory to God?

11. In what ways does this lesson's Bible passage challenge you to change the way you serve in the church?

LIFE LESSONS

Depending on our church background, we may have experienced anything from a complete avoidance of spiritual gifts to an overemphasis on them. We may immediately identify with the "ignorance" about gifts that Paul mentions in 1 Corinthians 12:1. Or we may feel confusion or even fear about gifts because we have seen them misused, misinterpreted, or abused. Paul reminds us that, like all of God's abundance of gifts, spiritual gifts have purposes and uses. They are meant to be part of the glue that holds the body of Christ together. God uses spiritual gifts to meet needs in our lives that we could never meet on our own. Identifying our gifts should increase our sense of responsibility, ministry, and purpose within the body of Christ. Our gifts should never be a reason for pride.

DEVOTION

God, we want only to please you. But fear and anxiety keep us from serving you well. Father, give us the confidence to recognize our spiritual gifts and the courage to use them for your glory. Thank you for the assurance that our imperfect service cannot stand in the way of your amazing power. We give you all the glory for what you accomplish through us.

For more Bible passages on spiritual gifts, see Romans 12:3–8; 1 Corinthians 7:7; 14:1–40; Ephesians 4:11–16; Hebrews 2:4; 1 Peter 4:10–11.

To complete the book of 1 Corinthians during this twelve-part study, read 1 Corinthians 12:1–11.

JOURNALING

In what ways have I personally benefited from the spiritual gifts of others?

THE BODY OF CHRIST

MAX LUCADO

REFLECTION

Unity in the church is something we all want but rarely experience. Think of a time when you felt a deep sense of unity among a group of believers. What were the contributing factors to that unity at that time? Consider some of the ways you were able to contribute to that sense of unity.

SITUATION

Once he highlighted the principle of spiritual gifts given by the Holy Spirit, Paul launched a major section that could be described as a spiritual anatomical lesson on the body of Christ. The gifts may be given to individuals, but their ultimate purpose, as we saw in the last lesson, is to benefit the entire body.

OBSERVATION

Read 1 Corinthians 12:12–26 from the NCV or the NKJV.

NCV

12A person's body is only one thing, but it has many parts. Though there are many parts to a body, all those parts make only one body. Christ is like that also. 13Some of us are Jews, and some are Greeks. Some of us are slaves, and some are free. But we were all baptized into one body through one Spirit. And we were all made to share in the one Spirit.

14The human body has many parts. 15The foot might say, "Because I am not a hand, I am not part of the body." But saying this would not stop the foot from being a part of the body. 16The ear might say, "Because I am not an eye, I am not part of the body." But saying this would not stop the ear from being a part of the body. 17If the whole body were an eye, it would not be able to hear. If the whole body were an ear, it would not be able to smell. 20So then there are many parts, but only one body.

21The eye cannot say to the hand, "I don't need you!" And the head cannot say to the foot, "I don't need you!" 22No! Those parts of the body that seem to be the weaker are really necessary. 23And the parts of the body we think are less deserving are the parts to which we give the most honor. We give special respect to the parts we want to hide. 24The more respectable parts of our body need no special care. But God put the body together and gave more honor to the parts that need it25so our body would not be divided. God wanted the different parts to care the same for each other. 26If one part of the body suffers, all the other parts suffer with it. Or if one part of our body is honored, all the other parts share its honor.

NKJV

12For as the body is one and has many members, but all the members of that one body, being many, are one body, so also is Christ. 13For by one Spirit we were all baptized into one body—whether Jews or Greeks, whether slaves or free—and have all been made to drink into one Spirit. 14For in fact the body is not one member but many.

15If the foot should say, "Because I am not a hand, I am not of the body," is it therefore not of the body? 16And if the ear should say, "Because I am not an eye, I am not of the body," is it therefore not of the body? 17If the whole body were an eye, where would be the hearing? If the whole were hearing, where would be the smelling? 18But now God has set the members, each one of them, in the body just as He pleased. 19And if they were all one member, where would the body be?

20But now indeed there are many members, yet one body. 21And the eye cannot say to the hand, "I have no need of you"; nor again the head to the feet, "I have no need of you." 22No, much rather, those members of the body which seem to be weaker are necessary. 23And those members of the body which we think to be less honorable, on these we bestow greater honor; and our unpresentable parts have greater modesty, 24but our presentable parts have no need. But God composed the body, having given greater honor to that part which lacks it, 25that there should be no schism in the body, but that the members should have the same care for one another. 26And if one member suffers, all the members suffer with it; or if one member is honored, all the members rejoice with it.

EXPLORATION

1. This passage compares the body of Christ to a human body. What observations have you made in thinking about that comparison and your personal experiences with the body of Christ?

Are very true + revealing. We seem to seek to be the most visible gifts. The hear the eyes - instead of really trying to seek what the Lord has for us! Many christians even now seem to think that the "tal" is of less importance than the head even in churches today -

Example - Mother Teresa" Sisters of Charity" Quote: God has not called us to be successful - but rather to be faithful."

2. In what ways are the various members of the church dependent on one another?

Can not function properly or heathly without each member doing their "own members part". The whole body suffers.

3. This Scripture warns against any part of the body considering itself either less important or more important than the others. What kind of parallel behavior in the church does this warn us about?

Less - Not completing "important" spiritual functions because "we" think their not as important! leaving a vacuum!

More - Letting pride come into our hearts!

4. Why did God give more honor to certain parts of the body of Christ?

Because it seems they are more critical in the function of the body but cannot function without the "lesser, so to seem" parts of the body.

5. We are to honor one another as parts of the same body. In light of this, how does God want us to treat one another? as equal - all having their own "important part to function properly, can't do with out each other to function properly." we should honor each other" we can all rejoice when one gets honored.

INSPIRATION

There was some dice-throwing that went on at the foot of the cross . . . I've wondered what that scene must have looked like to Jesus. As he looked downward past his bloody feet at the circle of gamblers, what did he think? What emotions did he feel? He must have been amazed. Here are common soldiers witnessing the world's most uncommon event and they don't know it. As far as they're concerned, it's just another Friday morning and he is just another criminal. "Come on. Hurry up; it's my turn!"

"All right, all right—this throw is for the sandals."

Casting lots for the possessions of Christ. Heads ducked. Eyes downward. Cross forgotten.

The symbolism is striking. Do you see it?

It makes me think of us. The religious. Those who claim heritage at the cross. I'm thinking of all of us. Every believer in the land. The stuffy. The loose. The strict. The simple. Upper church. Lower church. "Spirit-filled." Millenialists. Evangelical. Political. Mystical. Literal. Cynical. Robes. Collars. Three-piece suits. Born-againers. Ameners.

I'm thinking of us.

I'm thinking that we aren't so unlike those soldiers. (I'm sorry to say.)

We, too, play games at the foot of the cross. We compete for members. We scramble for status. We deal our judgments and condemnations. Competition. Selfishness. Personal gain. It's all there. We don't like what the other did so we take the sandal we won and walk away in a huff.

So close to the timbers yet so far from the blood.

We are so close to the world's most uncommon event, but we act like common crapshooters huddled in bickering groups and fighting over silly opinions.

How many pulpit hours have been wasted on preaching the trivial? How many churches have tumbled at the throes of miniscuity? How many leaders have saddled their pet peeves, drawn their swords of bitterness and launched into battle against brethren over issues that are not worth discussing?

So close to the cross but so far from the Christ.

We specialize in "I am right" rallies. We write books about what the other does wrong. We major in finding gossip and become experts in unveiling weaknesses. We split into little huddles and then, God forbid, we split again . . .

Are our differences that divisive? Are our opinions that obtrusive? Are our walls that wide? Is it *that* impossible to find a common cause?

"May they all be one," Jesus prayed.

One. Not one in groups of two thousand. But one in One. *One* church. *One* faith. *One* Lord. Not Baptist, not Methodist, not Adventist. Just Christian. No denominations. No hierarchies. No traditions. Just Christ.

Too idealistic? Impossible to achieve? I don't think so. Harder things have been done, you know. For example, once upon a tree, a Creator gave his life for his creation. Maybe all we need are a few hearts that are willing to follow suit. (From *No Wonder They Call Him the Savior* by Max Lucado)

Next wk.

REACTION

6. Why should we resist the temptation to compete with or compare ourselves to other believers? (See 2 Corinthians 10:12 for suggestions.)

7. In what ways do petty arguments and divisions in the church tarnish the gospel message?

8. How can we learn to appreciate each other's differences instead of allowing them to divide us?

9. What threatens the unity of your local church?

10. What steps can you take to promote peace and harmony in your church?

11. In what ways can you honor someone in your church who may feel unappreciated or insignificant?

LIFE LESSONS

Paul's lesson in anatomy points us in a healthy direction. Our advances in biology and medicine today allow us to marvel at how accurate the illustration proves to be. In fact, if we think about the principles in this passage at the cellular level, its impact deepens. We're almost tempted to think that an organ or an eye could function on its own. But a single cell isolated from the body cannot survive. We need one another. Followers of Jesus face a serious choice. When it comes to our individual relationship with the rest of the body of Christ, the question isn't *if* we will be involved with the rest of the body but *how* we will participate in the body.

DEVOTION

Father, we know that disputes and divisions don't belong in the body of Christ. But sometimes we hold on to our hurts, waiting for others to take the first step toward reconciliation. Give us courage, Father, to swallow our pride and reach out in love to our Christian brothers and sisters. Help us to look past our differences and focus on the common ground we share in you.

For more Bible passages on the body of Christ, see Romans 12:4–6; 1 Corinthians 14:4–26; Ephesians 4:25; 5:23–32; Colossians 1:18, 24–25.

To complete the book of 1 Corinthians during this twelve-part study, read 1 Corinthians 12:12–31.

JOURNALING

Since I'm a contributing member of the body of Christ, what can I do to help the body of Christ function most effectively?

TRUE LOVE

MAX
LUCADO

REFLECTION

Think for a few moments about the words you use to qualify love. Since we use the word *love* in so many settings, the meaning can get blurred. Consider how you might use that word more thoughtfully. To start, how does it feel to receive an extravagant present from someone you love? How does the love between you make it special?

SITUATION

Like a precious volume between two practical bookends, 1 Corinthians 13 is nestled into Paul's letter. This chapter is among the most recognized passages in Scripture, and it can stand alone as a beautiful tribute to God's love. But Paul wrote it as a crucial interlude between sections on the functioning of the body of Christ. In chapters 12 and 14 he was discussing the organic nature of the church. In chapter 13 he focused on the life that should permeate the church.

OBSERVATION

Read 1 Corinthians 13:1–13 from the NCV or the NKJV.

NCV

¹I may speak in different languages of people or even angels. But if I do not have love, I am only a noisy bell or a crashing cymbal. ²I may have the gift of prophecy. I may understand all the secret things of God and have all knowledge, and I may have faith so great I can move mountains. But even with all these things, if I do not have love, then I am nothing. ³I may give away everything I have, and I may even give my body as an offering to be burned. But I gain nothing if I do not have love.

⁴Love is patient and kind. Love is not jealous, it does not brag, and it is not proud. ⁵Love is not rude, is not selfish, and does not get upset with others. Love does not count up wrongs that have been done. ⁶Love is not happy with evil but is happy with the truth. ⁷Love patiently accepts all things. It always trusts, always hopes, and always remains strong.

⁸Love never ends. There are gifts of prophecy, but they will be ended. There are gifts of speaking in different languages, but those gifts will stop. There is the gift of knowledge, but it will come to an end. ⁹The reason is that our knowledge and our ability to prophesy are not perfect. ¹⁰But when perfection comes, the things that are not perfect will end. ¹¹When I was a child, I talked like a child, I thought like a child, I reasoned like a child. When I became a man, I stopped those childish ways. ¹²It is the same with us. Now we see a dim reflection, as if we were looking into a mirror, but then we shall see clearly. Now I know only a part, but then I will know fully, as God has known me. ¹³So these three things continue forever: faith, hope, and love. And the greatest of these is love.

NKJV

¹Though I speak with the tongues of men and of angels, but have not love, I have become sounding brass or a clanging cymbal. ²And though I have the gift of prophecy, and understand all mysteries and all knowledge, and though I have all faith, so that I could remove mountains, but have not love, I am nothing. ³And though I bestow all my goods to feed the poor, and though I give my body to be burned, but have not love, it profits me nothing.

⁴Love suffers long and is kind; love does not envy; love does not parade itself, is not puffed up; ⁵does not behave rudely, does not seek its own, is not provoked, thinks no evil; ⁶does not rejoice in iniquity, but rejoices in the truth; ⁷bears all things, believes all things, hopes all things, endures all things.

⁸Love never fails. But whether there are prophecies, they will fail; whether there are tongues, they will cease; whether there is knowledge, it will vanish away. ⁹For we know in part and we prophesy in part. ¹⁰But when that which is perfect has come, then that which is in part will be done away.

¹¹When I was a child, I spoke as a child, I understood as a child, I thought as a child; but when I became a man, I put away childish things. ¹²For now we see in a mirror, dimly, but then face to face. Now I know in part, but then I shall know just as I also am known.

¹³And now abide faith, hope, love, these three; but the greatest of these is love.

EXPLORATION

1. Even the best gifts are worthless if they aren't given in love. Why?

2. How can spiritual gifts be wasted? How can we help one another avoid gift-wastefulness?

3. This passage describes love with words such as *patient, kind, accepting,* and *trusting.* What can you add to that list?

4. What does true love require of us?

5. The love described in this passage is selfless and always faithful. Why is it difficult to demonstrate that kind of love?

INSPIRATION

More than one person has hailed 1 Corinthians 13 as the finest chapter in the Bible. No words get to the heart of loving people like these verses. And no verses get to the heart of the chapter like verses 4 through 8.

"Love is patient, love is kind. It does not envy, it does not boast, it is not proud. It is not rude, it is not self-seeking, it is not easily angered, it keeps no record of wrongs. Love does not delight in evil but rejoices with the truth. It always protects, always trusts, always hopes, always perseveres. Love never fails. But where there are prophecies, they will cease; where there are tongues, they will be stilled; where there is knowledge, it will pass away" (NIV).

Several years ago someone challenged me to replace the word *love* in this passage with my name. I did and became a liar. "Max is patient, Max is kind. Max does not envy, he does not boast, he is not proud . . ." That's enough! Stop right there! Those words are false. Max is not patient. Max is not kind. Ask my wife and kids. Max can be an out-and-out clod! That's my problem.

And for years that was my problem with this paragraph. It set a standard I could not meet. No one can meet it. No one, that is, except Christ. Does this passage not describe the measureless love of God? Let's insert Christ's name in place of the word *love* and see if it rings true.

"Jesus is patient, Jesus is kind. Jesus does not envy, Jesus does not boast, Jesus is not proud. Jesus is not rude, he is not self-seeking, he is not easily angered, he keeps no record of wrongs. Jesus does not delight in evil but rejoices with the truth. Jesus always protects, always trusts, always hopes, always perseveres. Jesus never fails."

Rather than let this Scripture remind us of a love we cannot produce, let it remind us of a love we cannot resist—God's love.

Some of you are so thirsty for this type of love. Those who should have loved you didn't. Those who could have loved you didn't. You were left at the hospital. Left at the altar. Left with an empty bed. Left with a broken heart. Left with your question, "Does anybody love me?"

Please listen to heaven's answer. God loves you. Personally. Powerfully. Passionately. Others have promised and failed. But God has promised and succeeded. He loves you with an unfailing love. And his love—if you will let it—can fill you and leave you with a love worth giving. (From *A Love Worth Giving* by Max Lucado)

REACTION

6. What sometimes keeps us from showing our love for others?

7. What can we learn from Christ's example about loving extravagantly and without limits? (See examples of Christ's love in Matthew 9:35–36; Mark 8:1–5; John 11:32–35.)

8. In what ways can God's love free us to love others?

9. Explain unconditional love.

10. When have you seen God's love transform a person?

11. In what ways can you extend God's love to someone today?

LIFE LESSONS

As we have seen, this chapter ultimately describes Jesus' love. It's not a love we can easily duplicate. It's a love we experience and then reflect. Some of our best moments in life come when we realize we have been channels of Jesus' love into someone else's life. We are simply passing on to others what was passed on to us.

DEVOTION

Father, the fact that you became flesh and dwelt among us proves that you love us far beyond our worth. We ask you, Father, to fill us to overflowing with your love, so that it flows freely from us to others. Let our lives be testimonies of your love so that when people look at us, they see a glimpse of your deep love for them.

For more Bible passages on love, see Matthew 5:43–46; Luke 6:35; John 13:34–35; Romans 5:5–8; Galatians 5:14; Ephesians 3:16–19; Hebrews 10:24; 1 Peter 1:22; 1 John 3:11–23.

To complete the book of 1 Corinthians during this twelve-part study, read 1 Corinthians 13:1–14:40.

JOURNALING

What are some ways I have felt God's love for me?

CHRIST'S VICTORY OVER DEATH

MAX LUCADO

REFLECTION

Human beings can be rather skittish when facing our mortality. Some people talk about it all the time; others do everything they can to avoid it. Think about what your friends believe about life after death. What comments have they made when an acquaintance or loved one has died? What conversations have you had with them about death? How do your beliefs differ?

SITUATION

As he ended the discussion on the logistics and details of worship, Paul made a natural transition back to the heart of his relationship with the Corinthians and the pulse of his ministry. It all rested on the risen Christ. He is aware that some "teachers" in Corinth have been promoting the idea that there is no resurrection from the dead (15:12). Paul knows that getting it wrong about Jesus' resurrection means getting it wrong about everything else. He launches an extended discussion of Jesus' resurrection and its crucial importance.

OBSERVATION

Read 1 Corinthians 15:20–34 from the NCV or the NKJV.

NCV

20But Christ has truly been raised from the dead—the first one and proof that those who sleep in death will also be raised. 21Death has come because of what one man did, but the rising from death also comes because of one man. 22In Adam all of us die. In the same way, in Christ all of us will be made alive again. 23But everyone will be raised to life in the right order. Christ was first to be raised. When Christ comes again, those who belong to him will be raised to life, 24and then the end will come. At that time Christ will destroy all rulers, authorities, and powers, and he will hand over the kingdom to God the Father. 25Christ must rule until he puts all enemies under his control. 26The last enemy to be destroyed will be death. 27The Scripture says that God put all things under his control. When it says "all things" are under him, it is clear this does not include God himself. God is the One who put everything under his control. 28After everything has been put under the Son, then he will put himself under God, who had put all things under him. Then God will be the complete ruler over everything.

29If the dead are never raised, what will people do who are being baptized for the dead? If the dead are not raised at all, why are people being baptized for them?

30And what about us? Why do we put ourselves in danger every hour? 31I die every day. That is true, brothers and sisters, just as it is true that I brag about you in Christ Jesus our Lord. 32If I fought wild animals in Ephesus only with human hopes, I have gained nothing. If the dead are not raised, "Let us eat and drink, because tomorrow we will die."

33Do not be fooled: "Bad friends will ruin good habits." 34Come back to your right way of thinking and stop sinning. Some of you do not know God—I say this to shame you.

NKJV

20But now Christ is risen from the dead, and has become the firstfruits of those who have fallen asleep. 21For since by man came death, by Man also came the resurrection of the dead. 22For as in Adam all die, even so in Christ all shall be made alive. 23But each one in his own order: Christ the firstfruits, afterward those who are Christ's at His coming. 24Then comes the end, when He delivers the kingdom to God the Father, when He puts an end to all rule and all authority and power. 25For He must reign till He has put all enemies under His feet. 26The last enemy that will be destroyed is death. 27For "He has put all things under His feet." But when He says "all things are put under Him," it is evident that He who put all things under Him is excepted. 28Now when all things are made subject to Him, then the Son Himself will also be subject to Him who put all things under Him, that God may be all in all.

²⁹*Otherwise, what will they do who are baptized for the dead, if the dead do not rise at all? Why then are they baptized for the dead?* ³⁰*And why do we stand in jeopardy every hour?* ³¹*I affirm, by the boasting in you which I have in Christ Jesus our Lord, I die daily.* ³²*If, in the manner of men, I have fought with beasts at Ephesus, what advantage is it to me? If the dead do not rise, "Let us eat and drink, for tomorrow we die!"*

³³*Do not be deceived: "Evil company corrupts good habits."* ³⁴*Awake to righteousness, and do not sin; for some do not have the knowledge of God. I speak this to your shame.*

EXPLORATION

1. This passage draws a comparison between Adam's death and Christ's death. What did the death of Christ give us that Adam's death didn't?

2. What proof do you see that there is life after death?

3. Sin entered the world when man sinned against God. How will Christ's death eventually destroy sin?

4. Believing there is life after death helped Paul face danger and endure hardship. How does that same belief help us face life? How does it help us face death?

5. What hope does Christ's resurrection offer? (For other Scriptures, see Romans 6:5; Philippians 3:10; 1 Peter 1:3.)

INSPIRATION

A sudden breeze, surprisingly warm, whistles through the leaves, scattering dust from the lifeless form. And with the breath of fresh air comes the difference. Winging on the warm wind is his image. Laughter is laid in the sculpted cheeks. A reservoir of tears is stored in the soul. A sprinkling of twinkle for the eyes. Poetry for the spirit. Logic. Loyalty. Like leaves on an autumn breeze, they float and land and are absorbed. His gifts become a part of him.

His Majesty smiles at his image. "It is good."

The eyes open.

Oneness. Creator and created walking on the river bank. Laughter. Purity. Innocent joy. Life unending.

Then the tree.

The struggle. The snake. The lie. The enticement. Heart torn, lured. Soul drawn to pleasure, to independence, to importance. Inner agony. Whose will?

The choice. Death of innocence. Entrance of death. The fall.

Tearstains mingling with fruit-stains . . .

[Then,] The Quest.

"Abram, you will father a nation! And Abram—tell the people I love them."

"Moses, you will deliver my people! And Moses—tell the people I love them."

"Joshua, you will lead the chosen ones! And Joshua—tell the people I love them."

"David, you will reign over the people! And David—tell the people I love them."

"Jeremiah, you will bear tidings of bondage! But Jeremiah, remind my children, remind my children that I love them."

Altars. Sacrifices. Rebelling. Returning. Reacting. Repenting. Romance. Tablets. Judges. Pillars. Bloodshed. Wars. Kings. Giants. Law. Hezekiah. Nehemiah. Hosea . . . God watching, never turning, ever loving, ever yearning for the Garden again . . .

[Finally,] empty throne. Spirit descending. Hushed angels.

A girl . . . a womb . . . an egg.

The same Divine Artist again forms a body. This time his own. Fleshly divinity. Skin layered on spirit. Omnipotence with hair. Toenails. Knuckles. Molars. Kneecaps. Once again he walks with man. Yet the Garden is now thorny. Thorns that cut, thorns that poison, thorns that remain lodged, leaving bitter wounds.

Disharmony. Sickness. Betrayal. Fear. Guilt.

The lions no longer pause. The clouds no longer hover. The birds scatter too quickly. Disharmony. Competition. Blindness.

And once again, a tree.

Once again the struggle. The snake. The enticement. Heart torn, lured. Once again the question, "Whose will?"

Then the choice. Tearstains mingle with bloodstains. Relationship restored. Bridge erected.

Once again he smiles. "It is good."

"For just as death came by the means of a man, in the same way the rising from death comes by means of a man. For just as all people die because of their union with Adam, in the same way all will be raised to life because of their union with Christ" (1 Corinthians 15:21–22 GNT). (From God Came Near by Max Lucado)

REACTION

6. What recurring theme is seen in the history of God's relationship with people?

7. Why did God send his Son to earth to die? (Before answering this question, consult these passages: Romans 5:6–8; Hebrews 9:27–29; 1 Peter 2:23–25.)

8. In what way is Christ's victory over death essential to our faith? (See also Romans 4:25; 5:12–19.)

9. In what ways would your life be different if you did not believe in life after death?

10. Describe what Christ's resurrection means to you.

11. How should the truth of this lesson's Bible passage affect the way you live today?

LIFE LESSONS

We might actually describe this passage as a collection of lessons on death that help us live life. People who deny, dismiss, or downplay the significance of Jesus' resurrection end up without an answer for their own deaths. Pull the resurrection of Jesus out of Christianity and the result is just another religious system with instructions for people trying to earn their way into God's favor or something even less significant. Those who accept the reality of Jesus' resurrection have good reasons to declare victory over death. Death still has to be faced, but it is a stingless death. Instead of being a cause for dread, death can be a motivation to gratitude. "But thanks be to God, who gives us the victory through our Lord Jesus Christ" (1 Cor. 15:57 NKJV).

DEVOTION

We praise you, Jesus, for conquering death for us. Your resurrection gives us hope that we will one day rise with you. Until that day, help us to remain faithful. Give us a glimpse into the everlasting so we will live for you no matter what the cost. May we see the joy that is before us, and may we set our hopes on spending eternity with you.

For more Bible passages on Christ's victory over death, see Isaiah 25:7–8; 53:10–12; John 5:24–29; Romans 4:25; 5:12–21; 2 Timothy 1:10; Hebrews 2:14–15.

To complete the book of 1 Corinthians during this twelve-part study, read 1 Corinthians 15:1–58.

JOURNALING

How can I know for certain that I will be raised with Christ?

GIVING TO
GOD'S WORK

MAX
LUCADO

REFLECTION

Think of a time when you have found great joy in giving to a charity or a church. Describe in three words your attitude about giving. How has giving been a source of blessing to you?

SITUATION

In the background of the book of Acts we find the church in Jerusalem experiencing financial straits. Some of these came as a result of early believers being cut off from their families. Others were caused by natural setbacks, droughts, and famines that affected the entire region. Paul and others encouraged the churches planted throughout the Mediterranean to reach out with help to the original church. Paul realized that his previous suggestions and encouragement must be followed up with specific instructions about giving.

OBSERVATION

Read 1 Corinthians 16:1–11 from the NCV or the NKJV.

NCV

¹Now I will write about the collection of money for God's people. Do the same thing I told the Galatian churches to do:²On the first day of every week, each one of you should put aside money as you have been blessed. Save it up so you will not have to collect money after I come. ³When I arrive, I will send whomever you approve to take your gift to Jerusalem. I will send them with letters of introduction, ⁴and if it seems good for me to go also, they will go along with me.

⁵I plan to go through Macedonia, so I will come to you after I go through there. ⁶Perhaps I will stay with you for a time or even all winter. Then you can help me on my trip, wherever I go. ⁷I do not want to see you now just in passing. I hope to stay a longer time with you if the Lord allows it. ⁸But I will stay at Ephesus until Pentecost, ⁹because a good opportunity for a great and growing work has been given to me now. And there are many people working against me.

¹⁰*If Timothy comes to you, see to it that he has nothing to fear with you, because he is working for the Lord just as I am.* ¹¹*So none of you should treat Timothy as unimportant, but help him on his trip in peace so that he can come back to me. I am expecting him to come with the brothers.*

NKJV

¹*Now concerning the collection for the saints, as I have given orders to the churches of Galatia, so you must do also:*²*On the first day of the week let each one of you lay something aside, storing up as he may prosper, that there be no collections when I come.* ³*And when I come, whomever you approve by your letters I will send to bear your gift to Jerusalem.* ⁴*But if it is fitting that I go also, they will go with me.*

⁵*Now I will come to you when I pass through Macedonia (for I am passing through Macedonia).* ⁶*And it may be that I will remain, or even spend the winter with you, that you may send me on my journey, wherever I go.* ⁷*For I do not wish to see you now on the way; but I hope to stay a while with you, if the Lord permits.*

⁸*But I will tarry in Ephesus until Pentecost.* ⁹*For a great and effective door has opened to me, and there are many adversaries.*

¹⁰*And if Timothy comes, see that he may be with you without fear; for he does the work of the Lord, as I also do.* ¹¹*Therefore let no one despise him. But send him on his journey in peace, that he may come to me; for I am waiting for him with the brethren.*

EXPLORATION

1. Paul advised the Corinthian church to collect money to support other Christians. In what ways do we follow Paul's advice today?

2. Paul instructed the Corinthians to save up their offering ahead of time rather than waiting until he came to start collecting. What was the advantage to this plan?

3. In what ways are the guidelines in this passage applicable to believers today?

4. What guidelines can we use to know how much money to give to the church? (For information on the principle of tithing, see Leviticus 27:30; Numbers 18:28; 2 Chronicles 31:5–6; Nehemiah 10:35–38.)

5. Timothy wasn't as prominent as Paul, yet Paul instructed the Corinthians to treat Timothy as an important person. Why?

INSPIRATION

You don't give for God's sake. You give for your sake. "The purpose of tithing is to teach you to always put God first in your lives" (Deut. 14:23 TLB). In what ways does tithing teach you? Consider the simple act of writing a check for the offering. First you enter the date. Already you are reminded that you are a time-bound creature and every possession you have will rust or burn. Best to give it while you can.

Then you enter the name of the one to whom you are giving the money. If the bank would cash it, you'd write God. But they won't, so you write the name of the church or group that has earned your trust.

Next comes the amount. Ahh, the moment of truth. You're more than a person with a checkbook. You're David, placing a stone in the sling. You're Peter, one foot on the boat, one foot on the lake. You're a little boy in a big crowd. A picnic lunch is all the Teacher needs, but it's all you have.

What will you do? Sling the Stone? Take the Step? Give the Meal?

Careful now, don't move too quickly. You aren't just entering an amount . . . you are making a confession. A confession that God owns it all anyway.

And then the line in the lower left-hand corner on which you write what the check is for. Hard to know what to put. It's for the light bills and literature. A little bit of outreach. A little bit of salary.

Better yet, it's partial payment for what the church has done to help you raise your family . . . keep your own priorities sorted out . . . tune you in to his ever-nearness.

Or, perhaps, best yet, it's for you. It's a moment for you to clip yet another strand from the rope of earth so that when he returns you won't be tied up. (From *When God Whispers Your Name* by Max Lucado)

REACTION

6. What are the purposes of tithing? How do you think it relates to other kinds of giving?

7. Think of a lesson you have learned through giving your money to God's work. Why does giving often result in a learning experience?

8. List some principles or "rules of the road" that can help you to be a better manager of God's money.

9. Explain why financial stewardship is important. Where does money/possessions management enter your relationship with God?

10. Why is it sometimes difficult to give generously to God's work?

11. Think of an improvement you could make, in light of this lesson's Bible passage, in the way you manage your money. How would that improvement change the way you give?

LIFE LESSONS

As stewards of certain possessions and means, we can practice both spontaneous and planned giving. We can be aware of unexpected needs that come up, practicing an attitude that declares we are ready to meet those needs as God supplies. But we can also plan and practice the discipline of systematic giving, including tithing and other giving that relates to ongoing needs. We can commit to supporting a missionary for a set monthly amount, expecting that God will help us meet that commitment. Money is an area in which God clearly tests our obedience, trust, and faithfulness.

DEVOTION

Father, you've been so good to us. Everything we have comes from your gracious hand. Forgive us, Father, for clinging too tightly to the things you have given us. Teach us to give generously and sacrificially to your work. Help us to put you first, in every area of our lives.

For more Bible passages on giving to God, see Genesis 28:22; Leviticus 27:30; Deuteronomy 15:10–11; Matthew 22:21; Acts 20:35; Romans 12:6–8; 2 Corinthians 9:7–15.

To complete the book of 1 Corinthians during this twelve-part study, read 1 Corinthians 16:1–24.

JOURNALING

What does my checkbook reveal to me about my priorities?

Lucado Life Lesson Series

Revised and updated, the Lucado Life Lessons series is perfect for small group or individual use and includes intriguing questions that will take you deeper into God's Word.

THOMAS NELSON
Since 1798

Available at your local Christian Bookstore.